A Book

There is no frigate like a book
To take us lands away,
Nor any coursers like a page
Of prancing poetry.
This traverse may the poorest take
Without oppress of toll;
How frugal is the chariot
That bears a human soul!

Emily Dickinson

The Paintbox

"Cobalt and umber and ultramarine,

Ivory black and emerald green —

What shall I paint to give pleasure to you?"

"Paint for me somebody utterly new."

"I have painted you tigers in crimson and white."

"The colors were good and you painted a-right."

"I have painted the cook and a camel in blue

And a panther in purple." "You painted them true.

Now mix me a color that nobody knows

And paint me a country where nobody goes

And put in it people a little like you,

Watching a unicorn drinking the dew."

E. V. Rieu

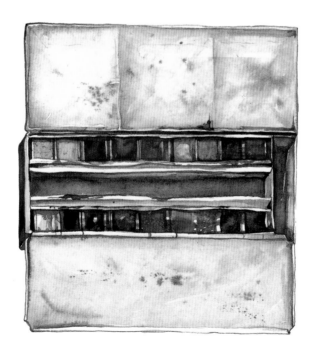

For Ffion and her dog, more lap dog than lone dog — J. M.

I would like to thank the friends who helped to form and shape this book. Tessa for the long nights poring over poetry books, all those who suggested favorite poems for inclusion, my children and Robin for their support, and I would like to dedicate "Fern Hill" to Colin Leyshon, who liked nothing more than to roll the words of poets around and had an enviable memory for poetry and song.

Barefoot Books
2067 Massachusetts Ave
Cambridge, MA 02140

Illustrations copyright © 2006 by Jackie Morris
Introduction copyright © 2006 by Carol Ann Duffy
The moral right of Jackie Morris to be identified as the illustrator
of this work has been asserted

This book has been printed on 100% acid-free paper

Graphic design by Sarah Hodder, London
Color separation by Bright Arts, Singapore
Printed and bound in China by Printplus Ltd
This book was typeset in Centaur/Centaur Italic
The illustrations were prepared in Winsor and Newton Artists' watercolor on Arches hot-pressed paper

Library of Congress Cataloging-in-Publication Data
Barefoot book of classic poems / Jackie Morris.
p. cm.
ISBN 1-905236-56-5 (acid-free paper)
1. Children's poetry, English. 2. Children's poetry, American. I. Morris, Jackie.
PR1175.3.B37 2006
821.008'09282—dc22
2005030379

1 3 5 7 9 8 6 4 2

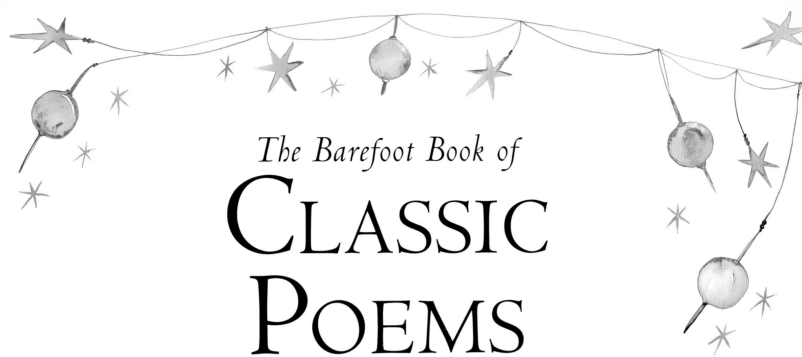

The Barefoot Book of
CLASSIC
POEMS

Compiled and illustrated by Jackie Morris

Introduced by Carol Ann Duffy

Barefoot Books
Celebrating Art and Story

Introduction

Here is the gorgeous *Barefoot Book of Classic Poems*, compiled
and beautifully illustrated by Jackie Morris. The poems
here are "classic" because, although their authors are no
longer living, they continue to shine brightly in the English
language — true stars. As E. V. Rieu's opening poem may
suggest, these are poems that persist in managing to be new.
This is an anthology for adults to rediscover, for children to
newly delight in, and for both to share together. It provides
a place, both magical and familiar, for our imaginations to
live in.

Some of the poems here are among the most enduring
children's poetry we have. They are almost part of our
DNA — "The Owl and the Pussy-Cat," "The Jabberwocky,"
"The Tyger," "maggie and milly and molly and may." The
rich illustrations to these familiar classics sing on the page, too.
Shakespeare, whose language remains the true expression of
our psyche, is here; along with Milton, Donne, Byron and
Wordsworth. Their poems read as vividly now as in the gone
days when they were written. Sylvia Plath, Stevie Smith and
Kathleen Raine are as powerfully present as Elizabeth Barrett
Browning, timelessly counting the ways in which she loves.
There are poems from the unique geniuses of Walt Whitman

and Dylan Thomas, whose glorious "Fern Hill" is the soul of childhood; from the War poets Isaac Rosenberg and Siegfried Sassoon; and from those formal masters, Byron and Auden. Throughout the book, there are real treasures to be found. There are surprising juxtapositions and deep echoes. As with all the best anthologies, the individual poems call and respond to each other across the pages and the ages.

Reading Jackie Morris's selection, what struck me forcibly was the truly *human* quality of the contents. From birth, when, as Sylvia Plath says, love sets us going like a fat gold watch, through childhood, to our relationship with the natural world, our journeys, love, war, belief and death, the poems open up real and imaginary ways of seeing, remembering or wondering. Poetry, of all the arts, offers us moments in language that preserve or celebrate, explore or elegize, transform or enhance our human joys and sadnesses. The best of poetry is memorable, as prayers are, and in this wonderful selection of classic poems both young and older readers will find something that will stay with them, or has stayed with them, all of their lives.

CAROL ANN DUFFY

Contents

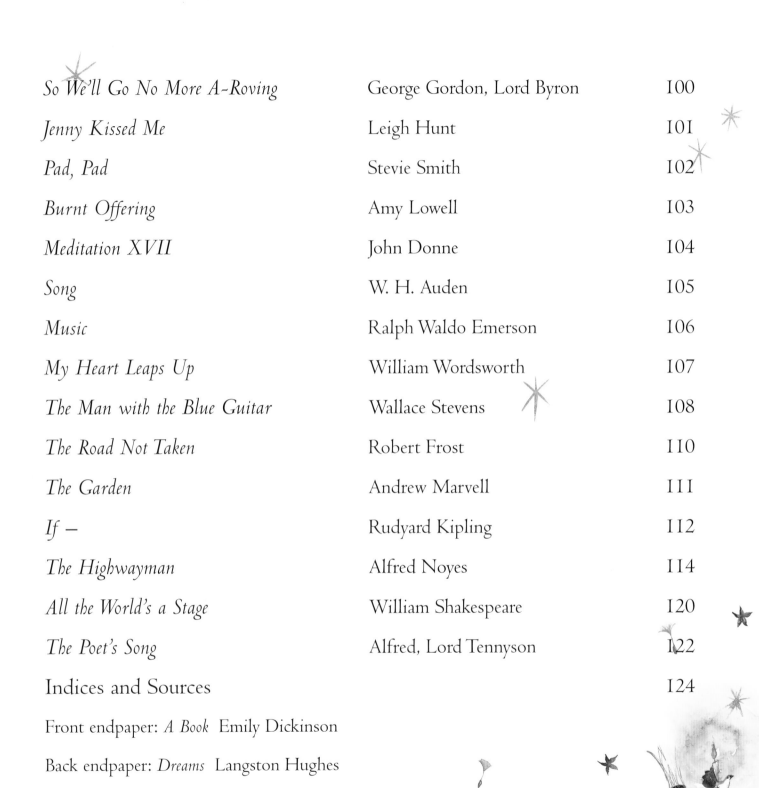

Front endpaper: *A Book* Emily Dickinson

Back endpaper: *Dreams* Langston Hughes

Spell of Creation

Within the flower there lies a seed,
Within the seed there springs a tree,
Within the tree there spreads a wood.

In the wood there burns a fire,
And in the fire there melts a stone,
Within the stone a ring of iron.

Within the ring there lies an O,
Within the O there looks an eye,
In the eye there swims a sea,

And in that sea reflected sky,
And in the sky there shines the sun,
Within the sun a bird of gold.

Within the bird there beats a heart,
And from the heart there flows a song,
And in the song there sings a word.

In the word there speaks a world,
A word of joy, a world of grief,
From joy and grief there springs my love.

Oh love, my love, there springs a world,
And on the world there shines a sun
And in the sun there burns a fire,

Within the fire consumes my heart
And in my heart there beats a bird,
And in the bird there wakes an eye,

Within the eye, earth, sea and sky,
Earth, sky and sea within an O
Lie like the seed within the flower.

Kathleen Raine

The Beautiful

Three things there are more beautiful
Than any man could wish to see:
The first, it is a full-rigged ship
Sailing with all her sails set free;
The second, when the wind and sun
Are playing in a field of corn;
The third, a woman young and fair,
Showing her child before it is born.

W. H. Davies

Morning Song

Love set you going like a fat gold watch.
The midwife slapped your footsoles, and your bald cry
Took its place among the elements.

Our voices echo, magnifying your arrival. New statue.
In a drafty museum, your nakedness
Shadows our safety. We stand round blankly as walls.

I'm no more your mother
Than the cloud that distils a mirror to reflect its own slow
Effacement at the wind's hand.

All night your moth-breath
Flickers among the flat pink roses. I wake to listen:
A far sea moves in my ear.

One cry, and I stumble from bed, cow-heavy and floral
In my Victorian nightgown.
Your mouth opens clean as a cat's. The window square

Whitens and swallows its dull stars. And now you try
Your handful of notes;
The clear vowels rise like balloons.

Sylvia Plath

New Child

Wait a while, small voyager
   On the shore, with seapinks and shells.

The boat
   Will take a few summers to build
That you must make your voyage in.

You will learn the names.
That golden light is "sun" — "moon"
   The silver light
That grows and dwindles.

And the beautiful small splinters
   That wet the stones, "rain."

There is a voyage to make,
   A chart to read,
But not yet, not yet.
   "Daisies" spill from your fingers.
   The night daisies are "stars."

The keel is laid, the strakes
   Will be set, in time.
A tree is growing
   That will be a tall mast.

All about you, meantime
The music of humanity,
   The dance of creation
Scored on the chart of the voyage.

The stories, legends, poems
Will be woven to make your sail.

You may hear the beautiful tale of Magnus
   Who took salt on his lip.
Your good angel
   Will be with you on that shore.

Soon, the voyage of EMMA
   To Tir-Nan-Og and beyond.

Star of the Sea, shine on her voyage.

George Mackay Brown

The Twins

In form and feature, face and limb,
I grew so like my brother,
That folks got taking me for him,
And each for one another.
It puzzled all our kith and kin,
It reached an awful pitch;
For one of us was born a twin,
Yet not a soul knew which.

One day (to make the matter worse),
Before our names were fixed,
As we were being wash'd by nurse
We got completely mixed;
And thus, you see, by Fate's decree,
(or rather nurse's whim),
My brother John got christened me,
And I got christened him.

This fatal likeness even dogg'd
My footsteps when at school,
And I was always getting flogg'd,
For John turned out a fool.
I put this question hopelessly
To everyone I knew —
What would you do, if you were me,
To prove that you were you?

Our close resemblance turned the tide
Of my domestic life;
For somehow my intended bride
Became my brother's wife.
In short, year after year the same
Absurd mistakes went on;
And when I died — the neighbours came
And buried brother John!

Henry S. Leigh

maggie and milly and molly and may

maggie and milly and molly and may
went down to the beach (to play one day)

and maggie discovered a shell that sang
so sweetly she couldn't remember her troubles, and

milly befriended a stranded star
whose rays five languid fingers were;

and molly was chased by a horrible thing
which raced sideways while blowing bubbles: and

may came home with a smooth round stone
as small as a world and as large as alone.

for whatever we lose (like a you or a me)
it's always ourselves we find in the sea

E. E. Cummings

Bed in Summer

In winter I get up at night
And dress by yellow candle-light.
In summer, quite the other way,
I have to go to bed by day.

I have to go to bed and see
The birds still hopping on the tree,
Or hear the grown-up people's feet
Still going past me in the street.

And does it not seem hard to you,
When all the sky is clear and blue,
And I should like so much to play,
To have to go to bed by day?

Robert Louis Stevenson

The Land of Counterpane

When I was sick and lay a-bed,
I had two pillows at my head,
And all my toys beside me lay
To keep me happy all the day.

And sometimes for an hour or so
I watched my leaden soldiers go,
With different uniforms and drills,
Among the bedclothes, through the hills;

And sometimes sent my ships in fleets
All up and down among the sheets;
Or brought my trees and houses out,
And planted cities all about.

I was the giant great and still
That sits upon the pillow-hill,
And sees before him, dale and plain,
The pleasant land of counterpane.

Robert Louis Stevenson

A Boy's Song

Where the pools are bright and deep,
Where the grey trout lies asleep,
Up the river and o'er the lea,
That's the way for Billy and me.

Where the blackbird sings the latest,
Where the hawthorn blooms the sweetest,
Where the nestlings chirp and flee,
That's the way for Billy and me.

Where the mowers mow the cleanest,
Where the hay lies thick and greenest,
There to trace the homeward bee,
That's the way for Billy and me.

Where the hazel bank is steepest,
Where the shadow falls the deepest,
Where the clustering nuts fall free,
That's the way for Billy and me.

Why the boys should drive away
Little sweet maidens from the play,
Or love to banter and fight so well,
That's the thing I never could tell.

But this I know, I love to play
Through the meadow, among the hay;
Up the water and over the lea,
That's the way for Billy and me.

James Hogg

A Spell for Sleeping

Sweet William, silverwood, sally-my-handsome.

Dimity darkens the pittering water.

On gloomed lawns wanders a king's daughter.

Curtains are clouding the casement windows.

A moon-glade smurrs the lake with light.

Doves cover the tower with quiet.

Three owls whit-whit in the withies.

Seven fish in a deep pool shimmer.

The princess moves to the spiral stair.

Slowly the sickle moon mounts up.

Frogs hump under moss and mushroom.

The princess climbs to her high hushed room,

Step by step to her shadowed tower.

Water laps the white lake shore.

A ghost opens the princess' door.

Seven fish in the sway of the water

Six candles for a king's daughter.

Five sighs for a drooping head.

Four ghosts to gentle her bed.

Three owls in the dusk falling.

Two tales to be telling.

One spell for sleeping.

Tamarisk, trefoil, tormentil.

Sleep rolls down from the clouded hill.

A princess dreams of a silver pool.

The moonlight spreads, the soft ferns flitter.

Stilled in a shimmering drift of water,

Seven fish dream of a lost king's daughter.

Alastair Reid

Annabel Lee

It was many and many a year ago,
In a kingdom by the sea,
That a maiden there lived whom you may know
By the name of ANNABEL LEE.
And this maiden she lived with no other thought
Than to love and be loved by me.

I was a child and she was a child
In this kingdom by the sea:
But we loved with a love that was more than love
I and my ANNABEL LEE,
With a love that the wingèd seraphs of heaven
Coveted her and me.

And this was the reason that, long ago,
In this kingdom by the sea,
A wind blew out of a cloud, chilling
My beautiful ANNABEL LEE,
So that her high-born kinsman came
And bore her away from me,
To shut her up in a sepulchre
In this kingdom by the sea.

The angels, not half so happy in heaven,
Went envying her and me —
Yes! That was the reason (as all men know,
In this kingdom by the sea)
That the wind came out of the cloud one night,
Chilling and killing my ANNABEL LEE.

But our love it was stronger by far than the love
Of those who were older than we —
Of many far wiser than we —
And neither the angels in heaven above,
Nor the demons down under the sea,
Can ever dissever my soul from the soul
Of the beautiful ANNABEL LEE:

For the moon never beams without bringing me dreams
Of the beautiful ANNABEL LEE;
And the stars never rise, but I feel the bright eyes
Of the beautiful ANNABEL LEE;
And so, all the night-tide, I lie down by the side
Of my darling — my darling — my life and my bride.
In the sepulchre there by the sea,
In her tomb by the sounding sea.

Edgar Allan Poe

Dorothy Dances

This is no child that dances. This is flame.

Here fire at last has found its natural frame.

What else is that which burns and flies

From those enkindled eyes…

What is that inner blaze

Which plays

About that lighted face…

This thing is fire set free —

Fire possesses her, or rather she

Controls its mastery.

With every gesture, every rhythmic stride,

Beat after beat,

It follows, purring at her side,

Or licks the shadows of her flashing feet.

Around her everywhere

It coils its thread of yellow hair;

Through every vein its bright blood creeps,

And its red hands

Caress her as she stands

Or lift her boldly when she leaps.

Then, as the surge of radiance grows stronger

These two are two no longer

And they merge

Into a disembodied ecstasy;

Free

To express some half-forgotten hunger,

Some half-forbidden urge.

What mystery

Has been at work until it blent

One child and that fierce element?

Give it no name.

It is enough that flesh has danced with fame.

Louis Untermeyer

The Stolen Child

Where dips the rocky highland
Of Sleuth Wood in the lake,
There lies a leafy island
Where flapping herons wake
The drowsy water rats;
There we've hid our faery vats,
Full of berries,
And of reddest stolen cherries.
Come away, O human child!
To the waters and the wild
With a faery, hand in hand,
For the world's more full of weeping than you can understand.

Where the wave of moonlight glosses
The dim grey sands with light,
Far off by furthest Rosses,
We foot it all the night,
Weaving olden dances
Mingling hands and mingling glances,
Till the moon has taken flight:
To and fro we leap
And chase the frothy bubbles,
While the world is full of troubles
And is anxious in its sleep.
Come away, O human child!
To the waters and the wild
With a faery, hand in hand,
For the world's more full of weeping than you can understand.

Where the wandering water gushes,

From the hills above Glen-Car,

In pools among the rushes

That scarce could bathe a star,

We seek for slumbering trout

And whispering in their ears

Give them unquiet dreams;

Leaning softly out

From ferns that drop their tears

Over the young streams.

Come away, O human child!

To the waters and the wild

With a faery, hand in hand,

For the world's more full of weeping than you can understand.

Away with us he's going,

The solemn-eyed:

He'll hear no more the lowing

Of the calves on the warm hillside

Or the kettle on the hob

Sing peace into his breast,

Or see the brown mice bob

Round and round the oatmeal chest.

For he comes, the human child,

To the waters and the wild

With a faery, hand in hand,

From a world more full of weeping than he can understand.

W. B. Yeats

33

The Wild Trees

O the wild trees of my home,
forests of blue dividing the pink moon,
the iron blue of those ancient branches
with their berries of vermilion stars.

In that place of steep meadows
the stacked sheaves are roasting,
and the sun-torn tulips
are tinders of scented ashes.

But here I have lost
the dialect of your hills,
my tongue has gone blind
far from their limestone roots.

Through trunks of black elder
runs a fox like a lantern,
and the hot grasses sing
with the slumber of larks.

But here there are thickets
of many different gestures,
torn branches of brick and steel
frozen against the sky.

O the wild trees of home
with their sounding dresses,
locks powdered with butterflies
and cheeks of blue moss.

I want to see you rise
from my brain's dry river,
I want your lips of wet roses
laid over my eyes.

O fountains of earth and rock,
gardens perfumed with cucumber,
home of secret valleys
where the wild trees grow.

Let me return at last
to your fertile wilderness,
to sleep with the coiled fernleaves
in your heart's live stone.

Laurie Lee

Tartary

If I were Lord of Tartary,
Myself and me alone,
My bed should be of ivory,
Of beaten gold my throne;
And in my court should peacocks flaunt,
And in my forests tigers haunt,
And in my pools great fishes slant
Their fins athwart the sun.

If I were Lord of Tartary,
Trumpeters every day
To all my meals should summon me,
And in my courtyards bray;
And in the evening lamps should shine
Yellow as honey, red as wine,
While harp and flute and mandoline
Made music sweet and gay.

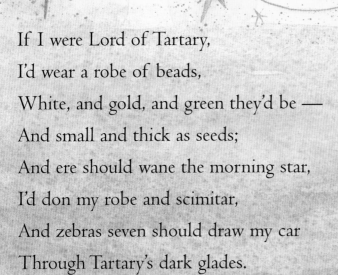

If I were Lord of Tartary,
I'd wear a robe of beads,
White, and gold, and green they'd be —
And small and thick as seeds;
And ere should wane the morning star,
I'd don my robe and scimitar,
And zebras seven should draw my car
Through Tartary's dark glades.

Lord of the fruits of Tartary,
Her rivers silver-pale!
Lord of the hills of Tartary,
Glen, thicket, wood and dale!
Her flashing stars, her scented breeze,
Her trembling lakes, like foamless seas,
Her bird-delighting citron-trees,
In every purple vale!

Walter de la Mare

Cats

Cats sleep
Anywhere,
Any table,
Any chair,
Top of piano,
Window-ledge,
In the middle,
On the edge,
Open drawer,
Empty shoe,
Anybody's
Lap will do.
Fitted in a
Cardboard box,
In a cupboard
With your frocks —
Anywhere.
They don't care!
Cats sleep
Anywhere.

Eleanor Farjeon

Furry Bear

If I were a bear,
And a big bear, too,
I shouldn't much care
If it froze or snew;
I shouldn't much mind
If it snowed or friz —
I'd be all fur-lined
With a coat like his!

For I'd have fur boots and a brown fur wrap,
And brown fur knickers and a big fur cap.
I'd have a fur muffle-ruff to cover my jaws,
And brown fur mittens on my big brown paws.

With a big brown furry-down up to my head,
I'd sleep all the winter in a big fur bed.

A. A. Milne

The Man in the Wilderness

The Man in the Wilderness asked of me,
"How many strawberries grow in the sea?"
I answered him, as I thought good,
"As many red herrings as grow in the wood."

The Man in the Wilderness asked me why
His hen could swim, and his pig could fly.
I answered him briskly, as I thought best,
"Because they were born in a cuckoo's nest."

The Man in the Wilderness asked me to tell
The sands in the sea, and I counted them well.
Says he with a grin, "And not one more?"
I answered him bravely, "You go and make sure."

Anon

The Answers

"When did the world begin and how?"
I asked a lamb, a goat, a cow:

"What's it all about and why?"
I asked a hog as he went by:

"Where will the whole thing end, and when?"
I asked a duck, a goose and a hen:

And I copied all the answers too,
A quack, a honk, an oink, a moo.

Robert Clairmont

The Jabberwocky

'Twas brillig, and the slithy toves
Did gyre and gimble in the wabe;
All mimsy were the borogoves,
And the mome raths outgrabe.

"Beware the Jabberwock, my son!
The jaws that bite, the claws that catch!
Beware the jubjub bird, and shun
The frumious bandersnatch!"

He took his vorpal sword in hand:
Long time the manxome foe he sought —
So rested he by the Tumtum tree
And stood awhile in thought.

And as in uffish thought he stood,
The Jabberwock, with eyes of flame,
Came whiffling through the tulgey wood,
And burbled as it came!

One, two! One, two! And through and through
The vorpal blade went snicker-snack!
He left it dead, and with its head
He went galumphing back.

"And hast thou slain the Jabberwock?
Come to my arms, my beamish boy!
O frabjous day! Callooh! Callay!"
He chortled in his joy.

'Twas brillig, and the slithy toves
Did gyre and gimble in the wabe;
All mimsy were the borogoves,
And the mome raths outgrabe.

Lewis Carroll

The Wild Swans at Coole

The trees are in their autumn beauty,
The woodland paths are dry,
Under the October twilight the water
Mirrors a still sky:
Upon the brimming water among the stones
Are nine-and-fifty swans.

The nineteenth autumn has come upon me
Since I first made my count;
I saw, before I had well finished,
All suddenly mount
And scatter wheeling in great broken rings
Upon their clamorous wings.

I have looked upon those brilliant creatures,
And now my heart is sore.
All's changed since I, hearing at twilight,
The first time on this shore,
The bell-beat of their wings above my head,
Trod with a lighter tread.

Unwearied still, lover by lover,
They paddle in the cold
Companionable streams or climb the air;
Their hearts have not grown old;
Passion or conquest, wander where they will,
Attend upon them still.

But now they drift on the still water,
Mysterious, beautiful;
Among what rushes will they build,
By what lakes edge or pool
Delight men's eyes when I awake some day
To find they have flown away?

W. B. Yeats

The Tale of Custard the Dragon

Belinda lived in a little white house,
With a little black kitten and a little gray mouse,
And a little yellow dog and a little red wagon,
And a realio, trulio, little pet dragon.

Now the name of the little black kitten was Ink,
And the little gray mouse, she called her Blink,
And the little yellow dog was as sharp as Mustard,
But the dragon was a coward, and she called him Custard.

Custard the dragon had big sharp teeth,
And spikes on top of him and scales underneath,
Mouth like a fireplace, chimney for a nose,
And realio, trulio, daggers on his toes.

Belinda was as brave as a barrel full of bears,
And Ink and Blink chased lions down the stairs.
Mustard was as brave as a tiger in a rage,
But Custard cried for a nice safe cage.

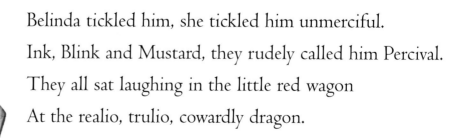

Belinda tickled him, she tickled him unmerciful.
Ink, Blink and Mustard, they rudely called him Percival.
They all sat laughing in the little red wagon
At the realio, trulio, cowardly dragon.

Belinda giggled till she shook the house,
And Blink said Weeck! which is giggling for a mouse,
Ink and Mustard rudely asked his age,
When Custard cried for a nice safe cage.

Suddenly, suddenly they heard a nasty sound,
And Mustard growled, and they all looked around.
Meowch! cried Ink, and Ooh! cried Belinda,
For there was a pirate, climbing in the winda!

Pistol in his left hand, pistol in his right,
And he held in his teeth a cutlass bright,
His beard was black, one leg was wood;
It was clear that the pirate meant no good.

Belinda paled, and she cried, "Help! Help!"
But Mustard fled with a terrified yelp,
Ink trickled down to the bottom of the household,
And little mouse Blink strategically mouseholed.

But up jumped Custard, snorting like an engine,
Clashed his tail like irons in a dungeon,
With a clatter and a clank and a jaggling squirm
He went at the pirate like a robin at a worm.

The pirate gaped at Belinda's dragon,
And gulped some grog from his pocket flagon,
He fired two bullets but they didn't hit,
And Custard gobbled him, every bit.

Belinda embraced him, Mustard licked him,
No one mourned for his pirate victim.
Ink and Blink in glee did gyrate
Around the dragon that ate the pyrate.

Belinda still lives in her little white house,
With her little black kitten and her little gray mouse,
And her little yellow dog and her little red wagon,
And her realio, trulio, little pet dragon.

Belinda is as brave as a barrel full of bears,
And Ink and Blink chase lions down the stairs,
Mustard is as brave as a tiger in a rage,
But Custard keeps crying for a nice safe cage.

Ogden Nash

The Owl and the Pussy-Cat

The Owl and the Pussy-Cat went to sea
    In a beautiful pea-green boat:
They took some honey, and plenty of money
    Wrapped up in a five-pound note.
The Owl looked up to the stars above,
    And sang to a small guitar,
"O lovely pussy, O Pussy, my love,
    What a beautiful Pussy you are,
        You are,
        You are!
What a beautiful Pussy you are!"

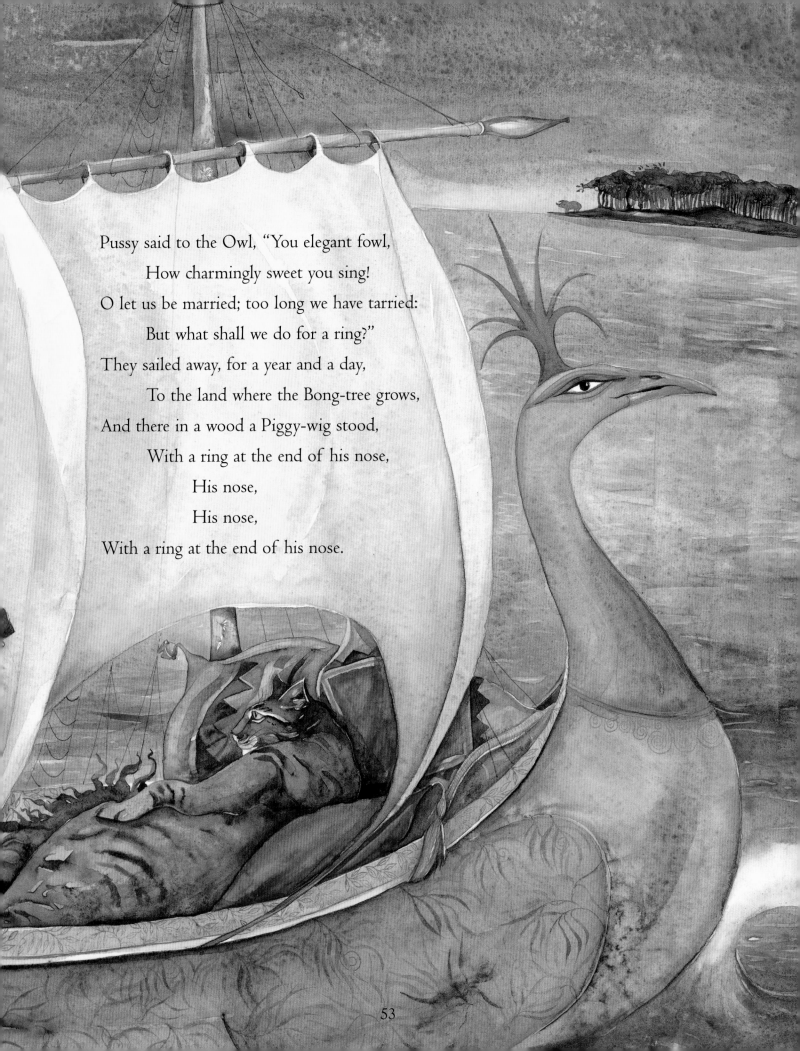

Pussy said to the Owl, "You elegant fowl,
    How charmingly sweet you sing!
O let us be married; too long we have tarried:
    But what shall we do for a ring?"
They sailed away, for a year and a day,
    To the land where the Bong-tree grows,
And there in a wood a Piggy-wig stood,
    With a ring at the end of his nose,
        His nose,
        His nose,
With a ring at the end of his nose.

"Dear Pig, are you willing to sell for one shilling

Your ring?" Said the Piggy, "I will."

So they took it away, and were married next day

By the Turkey who lives on the hill.

They dined on mince, and slices of quince,

Which they ate with a runcible spoon;

And hand in hand, on the edge of the sand,

They danced by the light of the moon,

The moon,

The moon,

They danced by the light of the moon.

Edward Lear

Something told the wild geese

Something told the wild geese
It was time to go,
Though the fields lay golden
Something whispered, "Snow!"
Leaves were green and stirring,
Berries lustre-glossed,
But beneath warm feathers
Something cautioned, "Frost!"

All the sagging orchards
Steamed with amber spice,
But each wild breast stiffened
At remembered ice.
Something told the wild geese
It was time to fly —
Summer sun was on their wings,
Winter in their cry.

Rachel Field

The Fish

wade

through black jade.

      Of the crow-blue mussel-shells, one keeps

      adjusting the ash-heaps;

         opening and shutting itself like

an

injured fan.

     The barnacles which encrust the side

     of the wave, cannot hide

        there for the submerged shafts of the

     sun,

     split like spun

        glass, move themselves with spotlight swiftness

        into the crevices —

         in and out, illuminating

the

turquoise sea

     of bodies. The water drives a wedge

     of iron throught the iron edge

        of the cliff; whereupon the stars,

pink

rice-grains, ink-

bespattered jelly fish, crabs like green

lilies, and submarine

toadstools, slide each on the other.

All

external

marks of abuse are present on this

defiant edifice —

all the physical features of

ac-

cident — lack

of cornice, dynamite grooves, burns, and

hatchet strokes, these things stand

out on it; the chasm-side is

dead.

Repeated

evidence has proved that it can live

on what can not revive

its youth. The sea grows old in it.

Marianne Moore

The Flower-Fed Buffaloes

The flower-fed buffaloes of the spring
In the days of long ago,
Ranged where the locomotives sing
And the prairie flowers lie low:—
The tossing, blooming, perfumed grass
Is swept away by wheat,
Wheels and wheels and wheels spin by
In the spring that still is sweet.
But the flower-fed buffaloes of the spring
Left us, long ago.
They gore no more, they bellow no more,
They trundle around the hills no more:—
With the Blackfeet, lying low,
With the Pawnees, lying low,
Lying low.

Vachel Lindsay

58

Oliphaunt

Grey as a mouse,

Big as a house,

Nose like a snake,

I make the earth shake,

As I tramp through the grass;

Trees crack as I pass.

With horns in my mouth,

I walk in the South,

Flapping big ears.

Beyond count of years

I stump round and round,

Never lie on the ground,

Not even to die.

Oliphaunt am I,

Biggest of all,

Huge, old, and tall.

If ever you'd met me

You wouldn't forget me.

If you never do,

You won't think I'm true;

But old Oliphaunt am I,

And never lie.

J. R. R. Tolkien

Pegasus

From the blood of Medusa
Pegasus sprang.
His hoof upon heaven
Like melody rang,
His whinny was sweeter
Than Orpheus' lyre,
The wing on his shoulder
Was brighter than fire.

His tail was a fountain
His nostrils were caves,
His mane and his forelock
Were musical waves,
He neighed like a trumpet,
He cooed like a dove,
He was stronger than terror
And swifter than love.

He could not be captured,
He could not be bought,
His running was rhythm,
His standing was thought;
With one eye on sorrow
And one eye on mirth,
He galloped in heaven
And gambolled on earth.

And only the poet
With wings to his brain
Can mount him and ride him
Without any rein.
The stallion of heaven,
The steed of the skies,
The horse of the singer
Who sings as he flies.

Eleanor Farjeon

The Birds

Do you ask what the birds say?
    The sparrow, the dove,
The linnet and thrush say:
    I love and I love.

In the Winter they're silent,
    The wind is so strong;
What it says I don't know
    But it sings a loud song.

But green leaves and blossoms,
    And sunny, warm weather,
And singing, and loving,
    All come back together.

But the lark is so brimful
    Of gladness and love,
The green fields below him,
    The blue sky above.

That he sings and he sings
    And forever sings he:
I love my love
And my love loves me.

Samuel Taylor Coleridge

The Donkey

When fishes flew and forests walked
    And figs grew upon thorn,
Some moment when the moon was blood
    Then surely I was born.

With monstrous head and sickening cry
    And ears like errant wings,
The devil's walking parody
    On all four-footed things.

The tattered outlaw of the earth,
    Of ancient crooked will;
Starve, scourge, deride me: I am dumb,
    I keep my secret still.

Fools! For I also had my hour,
    One far fierce hour and sweet:
There was a shout about my ears,
    And palms before my feet.

G. K. Chesterton

Lobster Quadrille

"Will you walk a little faster?" said a whiting to a snail.

"There's a porpoise close behind us, and he's treading on my tail.

See how eagerly the lobsters and the turtles all advance!

They are waiting on the shingle — will you come and join the dance?

Will you, won't you, will you, won't you, will you join the dance?

Will you, won't you, will you, won't you, won't you join the dance?"

"You can really have no notion how delightful it will be,

When they take us up and throw us, with the lobsters, out to sea!"

But the snail replied "Too far, too far!" and gave a look askance —

Said he thanked the whiting kindly, but he would not join the dance.

Would not, could not, would not, could not, would not join the dance.

Would not, could not, would not, could not, could not join the dance.

"What matters it how far we go?" his scaly friend replied.

"There is another shore, you know, upon the other side.

The further off from England the nearer is to France —

Then turn not pale, beloved snail, but come and join the dance.

 Will you, won't you, will you, won't you, will you join the dance?

 Will you, won't you, will you, won't you, won't you join the dance?"

Lewis Carroll

Lone Dog

I'm a lean dog, a keen dog, a wild dog and lone;

I'm a rough dog, a tough dog, hunting on my own;

I'm a bad dog, a mad dog, teasing silly sheep,

I love to sit and bay the moon, to keep fat souls from sleep.

I'll never be a lap dog, licking dirty feet.

A sleek dog, a meek dog, cringing for my meat;

Not for me the fireside, the well-filled plate,

But shut door, and sharp stone, and cuff and kick and hate.

Not for me the other dogs, running by my side,

Some have run a short while, but none of them would bide;

O mine is the still lone trail, the hard trail, the best,

Wide wind, and wild stars, and the hunger of the quest.

Irene McCleod

The Panther

His vision, from the constantly passing bars,

has grown so weary that it cannot hold

anything else. It seems to him there are

a thousand bars; and behind the bars, no world.

As he paces in cramped circles, over and over,

the movement of his powerful soft strides

is like a ritual dance around a center

in which a mighty will stands paralyzed.

Only at times, the curtain of the pupils

lifts, quietly. An image enters in,

rushes down through the tense, arrested muscles,

plunges into the heart and is gone.

Rainer Maria Rilke

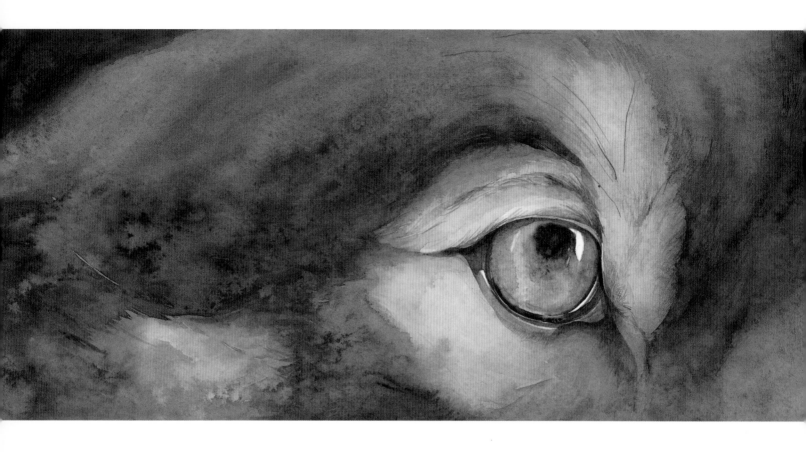

Amulet

Inside the Wolf's fang, the mountain of heather.

Inside the mountain of heather, the Wolf's fur.

Inside the Wolf's fur, the ragged forest.

Inside the ragged forest, the Wolf's foot.

Inside the Wolf's foot, the stony horizon.

Inside the stony horizon, the Wolf's tongue.

Inside the Wolf's tongue, the Doe's tears.

Inside the Doe's tears, the frozen swamp.

Inside the frozen swamp, the Wolf's blood.

Inside the Wolf's blood, the snow wind.

Inside the snow wind, the Wolf's eye.

Inside the Wolf's eye, the North Star.

Inside the North Star, the Wolf's fang.

Ted Hughes

The Tyger

Tyger! Tyger! burning bright
In the forests of the night,
What immortal hand or eye
Could frame thy fearful symmetry?

In what distant deeps or skies
Burnt the fire of thine eyes?
On what wings dare he aspire?
What the hand, dare seize the fire?

And what shoulder, and what art,
Could twist the sinews of thy heart?
And when thy heart began to beat,
What dread hand? and what dread feet?

What the hammer? what the chain?
In what furnace was thy brain?
What the anvil? what dread grasp
Dare its deadly terrors clasp?

When the stars threw down their spears
And watered Heaven with their tears,
Did he smile his work to see?
Did he who made the Lamb make thee?

Tyger! Tyger! burning bright
In the forests of the night,
What immortal hand or eye
Dare frame thy fearful symmetry?

William Blake

Windy Nights

Whenever the moon and stars are set,
Whenever the wind is high,
All night long in the dark and wet,
A man goes riding by.
Late in the night when the fires are out,
Why does he gallop and gallop about?

Whenever the trees are crying aloud,
And ships are tossed at sea,
By, on the highway, low and loud,
By at the gallop goes he.
By at the gallop he goes, and then
By he comes back at the gallop again.

Robert Louis Stevenson

Moonlit Apples

At the top of the house the apples are laid in rows,
And the skylight lets the moonlight in, and those
Apples are deep-sea apples of green. There goes
    A cloud on the moon in the autumn night.

A mouse in the wainscot scratches, and scratches, and then
There is no sound at the top of the house of men
Or mice; and the cloud is blown, and the moon again
    Dapples the apples with deep-sea light.

They are lying in rows there, under the gloomy beams,
On the sagging floor; they gather the silver streams
Out of the moon, those moonlit apples of dreams,
    And quiet is the steep stair under.

In the corridors under there is nothing but sleep.
And stiller than ever on orchard boughs they keep
Tryst with the moon, and deep is the silence, deep
    On moon-washed apples of wonder.

John Drinkwater

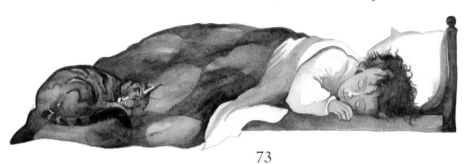

Daffodils

I wandered lonely as a cloud
That floats on high o'er vales and hills,
When all at once I saw a crowd,
A host, of golden daffodils.
Beside the lake, beneath the trees,
Fluttering and dancing in the breeze.

Continuous as the stars that shine
And twinkle on the milky way,
They stretched in never-ending line
Along the margin of a bay:
Ten thousand saw I at a glance
Tossing their heads in sprightly dance.

The waves beside them danced, but they
Out-did the sparkling waves in glee:
A poet could not but be gay
In such a jocund company!
I gazed — and gazed — but little thought
What wealth the show to me had brought:

For oft, when on my couch I lie
In vacant or in pensive mood,
They flash upon that inward eye
Which is the bliss of solitude;
And then my heart with pleasure fills,
And dances with the daffodils.

William Wordsworth

75

from *Song of Myself*

I celebrate myself, and sing myself,
And what I assume you shall assume,
For every atom belonging to me as good belongs to you.

I loafe and invite my soul,
I lean and loafe at my ease observing a spear of summer grass.

My tongue, every atom of my blood, form'd from this soil, this air,
Born here of parents born here from parents the same, and their parents the same,
I, now thirty-seven years old in perfect health begin,
Hoping to cease not till death.
Creeds and schools in abeyance,
Retiring back a while sufficed at what they are, but never forgotten,
I harbor for good or bad, I permit to speak at every hazard,
Nature without check with original energy.

Walt Whitman

Fern Hill

Now as I was young and easy under the apple boughs
About the lilting house and happy as the grass was green,
    The night above the dingle starry,
      Time let me hail and climb
    Golden in the heydays of his eyes,
And honoured among wagons I was prince of the apple towns
And once below a time I lordly had the trees and leaves
      Trail with daisies and barley
    Down the rivers of the windfall light.

And as I was green and carefree, famous among the barns
About the happy yard and singing as the farm was home,
    In the sun that is young once only,
      Time let me play and be
    Golden in the mercy of his means,
And green and golden I was huntsman and herdsman, the calves
Sang to my horn, the foxes on the hills barked clear and cold,
      And the sabbath rang slowly
    In the pebbles of the holy streams.

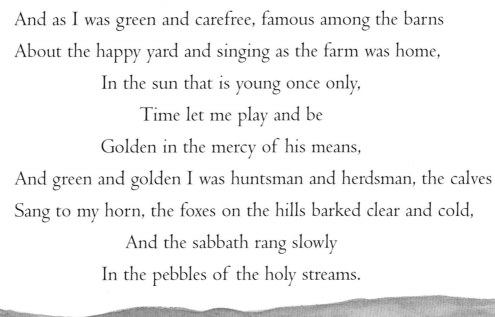

All the sun long it was running, it was lovely, the hay

Fields high as the house, the tunes from the chimneys, it was air

And playing, lovely and watery

And fire green as grass.

And nightly under the simple stars

As I rode to sleep the owls were bearing the farm away,

All the moon long I heard, blessed among stables, the night-jars

Flying with the ricks, and the horses

Flashing into the dark.

And then to awake, and the farm, like a wanderer white

With the dew, come back, the cock on his shoulder: it was all

Shining, it was Adam and maiden,

The sky gathered again

And the sun grew round that very day.

So it must have been after the birth of the simple light

In the first, spinning place, the spellbound horses walking warm

Out of the whinnying green stable

On to the fields of praise.

And honoured among foxes and pheasants by the gay house
Under the new made clouds and happy as the heart was long,
    In the sun born over and over,
        I ran my heedless ways,
    My wishes raced through the house high hay
And nothing I cared, at my sky blue trades, that time allows
In all his tuneful turning so few and such morning songs
        Before the children green and golden
            Follow him out of grace,

Nothing I cared, in the lamb white days, that time would take me
Up to the swallow thronged loft by the shadow of my hand,
        In the moon that is always rising,
            Nor that riding to sleep
    I should hear him fly with the high fields
And wake to the farm forever fled from the childless land.
Oh as I was young and easy in the mercy of his means,
            Time held me green and dying
        Though I sang in my chains like the sea.

                                    Dylan Thomas

Until I Saw the Sea

Until I saw the sea
I did not know
that wind
could wrinkle water so.

I never knew
that sun
could splinter a whole sea of blue.

Nor
did I know before
a sea breathes in and out
upon a shore.

Lilian Moore

The Night Mail

This is the night mail crossing the border,

Bringing the cheque and the postal order,

Letters for the rich, letters for the poor,

The shop at the corner and the girl next door,

Pulling up Beattock, a steady climb —

The gradient's against her, but she's on time.

Past cotton grass and moorland boulder,

Shoveling white steam over her shoulder,

Snorting noisily as she passes

Silent miles of wind-bent grasses;

Birds turn their heads as she approaches,

Stare from the bushes at her blank-faced coaches;

Sheepdogs cannot turn her course,

They slumber on with paws across;

In the farm she passes no one wakes

But a jug in the bedroom gently shakes.

Dawn freshens, the climb is done.

Down towards Glasgow she descends

Towards the steam tugs yelping down the glade of cranes

Towards the fields of apparatus, the furnaces

Set on the dark plain like gigantic chessmen.

All Scotland waits for her;

In the dark glens, beside the pale-green sea lochs,

Men long for news.

Letters of thanks, letters from banks,
Letters of joy from the girl and boy,
Receipted bills and invitations
To inspect new stock or visit relations,
And applications for situations,
And timid lovers' declarations,
And gossip, gossip from all the nations,
News circumstantial, news financial,
Letters with holiday snaps to enlarge in,
Letters with faces scrawled in the margin.
Letters from uncles, cousins and aunts,
Letters to Scotland from the South of France,
Letters of condolence to Highlands and Lowlands,
Notes from overseas to Hebrides;
Written on paper of every hue,
The pink, the violet, the white and the blue,
The chatty, the catty, the boring, adoring,
The cold and official and the heart's outpouring.
Clever, stupid, short and long,
The typed and printed and the spelt all wrong.

Thousands are still asleep
Dreaming of terrifying monsters
Or a friendly tea beside the band at Cranston's or Crawford's;
Asleep in working Glasgow, asleep in well-set Edinburgh,
Asleep in granite Aberdeen.
They continue their dreams
But shall wake soon and long for letters.
And none will hear the postman's knock
Without a quickening of the heart,
For who can bear to feel himself forgotten?

W. H. Auden

83

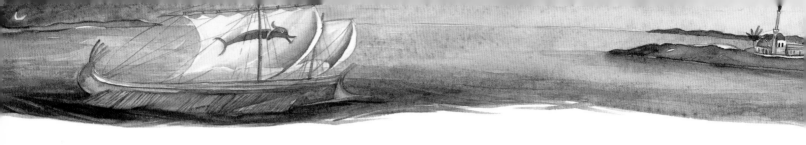

Cargoes

Quinquireme of Nineveh from distant Ophir
Rowing home to haven in sunny Palestine,
With a cargo of ivory,
And apes and peacocks,
Sandalwood, cedarwood, and sweet white wine.

Stately Spanish galleon coming from the Isthmus,
Dipping through the Tropics by the palm-green shores,
With a cargo of diamonds,
Emeralds, amethysts,
Topazes, and cinnamon, and gold moidores.

Dirty British coaster with a salt-caked smoke stack
Butting through the Channel in the mad March days,
With a cargo of Tyne coal,
Road-rail, pig-lead,
Firewood, iron-ware, and cheap tin trays.

John Masefield

Recuerdo

We were very tired, we were very merry —
We had gone back and forth all night on the ferry.
It was bare and bright, and smelled like a stable —
But we looked into a fire, we leaned across a table,
We lay on a hill-top underneath the moon;
And the whistles kept blowing and the dawn came soon.

We were very tired, we were very merry —
We had gone back and forth all night on the ferry.
And you ate an apple, and I ate a pear,
From a dozen of each we had bought somewhere;
And the sun went wan, and the wind came cold,
And the sun rose dripping, a bucketful of gold.

We were very tired, we were very merry —
We had gone back and forth all night on the ferry.
We hailed, "Good morning, mother!" to a shawl-covered head,
And bought a morning paper, which neither of us read;
And she wept, "God bless you!" for the apples and pears,
And we gave her all our money but our subway fares.

Edna St. Vincent Millay

She Walks in Beauty

She walks in beauty, like the night
   Of cloudless chimes and starry skies;
And all that's best of dark and bright
   Meet in her aspect and her eyes:
Thus mellow'd to that tender light
   Which heaven to gaudy day denies.

One shade the more, one ray the less,
   Had half impair'd the nameless grace
Which waves in every raven tress,
   Or softly lightens o'er her face;
Where thoughts serenely sweet express
   How pure, how dear their dwelling place.

And on that cheek, and o'er that brow,
   So soft, so calm, yet eloquent,
The smiles that win, the tints that glow,
   But tell of days in goodness spent,
A mind at peace with all below,
   A heart whose love is innocent!

George Gordon, Lord Byron

He Wishes for the Cloths of Heaven

Had I the heavens' embroidered cloths,
Enwrought with golden and silver light,
The blue and the dim and the dark cloths
Of night and light and the half-light,
I would spread the cloths under your feet:
But I, being poor, have only my dreams;
I have spread my dreams under your feet;
Tread softly because you tread on my dreams.

W. B. Yeats

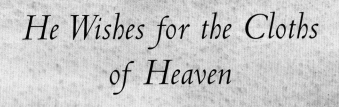

How Do I Love Thee?

How do I love thee? Let me count the ways.
I love thee to the depth and breadth and height
My soul can reach, when feeling out of sight
For the ends of Being and ideal Grace.
I love thee to the level of everyday's
Most quiet need, by sun and candle-light.
I love thee freely, as men strive for Right;
I love thee purely, as they turn from Praise.
I love thee with the passion put to use
In my old griefs, and with my childhood's faith.
I love thee with a love I seemed to lose
With my lost saints, — I love thee with the breath,
Smiles, tears, of all my life! — and, if God choose,
I shall but love thee better after death.

Elizabeth Barrett Browning

Sonnet 18

Shall I compare thee to a summer's day?

Thou art more lovely and more temperate:

Rough winds do shake the darling buds of May,

And summer's lease hath all too short a date;

Sometimes too hot the eye of heaven shines,

And often is his gold complexion dimmed;

And every fair from fair sometime declines,

By chance or nature's changing course untrimmed:

But thy eternal summer shall not fade,

Nor lose possession of that fair thou ow'st;

Nor shall death brag thou wander'st in his shade,

When in eternal lines to time thou grow'st:

    So long as men can breathe, or eyes can see,

    So long lives this, and this gives life to thee.

William Shakespeare

A Birthday

My heart is like a singing bird

    Whose nest is in a watered shoot;

My heart is like an apple tree

    Whose boughs are bent with thickset fruit;

My heart is like a rainbow shell

    That paddles in a halcyon sea;

My heart is gladder than all these

    Because my love is come to me.

Raise me a dais of silk and down;

    Hang it with vair and purple dyes;

Carve it in doves and pomegranates,

    And peacocks with a hundred eyes;

Work it in gold and silver grapes,

    In leaves and silver fleurs-de-lys;

Because the birthday of my life

    Is come, my love is come to me.

Christina Rossetti

This Is Just To Say

I have eaten

the plums

that were in

the icebox

and which

you were probably

saving

for breakfast

Forgive me

they were delicious

so sweet

and so cold

William Carlos Williams

The War Song of Dinas Vawr

The mountain sheep are sweeter,
But the valley sheep are fatter;
We therefore deemed it meeter
To carry off the latter.
We made an expedition;
We met a host, and quelled it;
We forced a strong position,
And killed the men who held it.

On Dyfed's richest valley,
Where herds of kine were browsing,
We made a mighty sally,
To furnish our carousing.
Fierce warriors rushed to meet us;
We met them, and o'erthrew them:
They struggled hard to beat us;
But we conquered them, and slew them.

As we drove our prize at leisure,
The king marched forth to catch us:
His rage surpassed all measure,
But his people could not match us.
He fled to his hall-pillars;
And, ere our force we led off,
Some sacked his house and cellars,
While others cut his head off.

We there, in strike bewildr'ing,
Spilt blood enough to swim in:
We orphaned many children,
And widowed many women.
The eagles and the ravens
We glutted with our foemen;
The heroes and the cravens,
The spearmen and the bowmen.

We brought away from battle,
And much their land bemoaned them,
Two thousand head of cattle,
And the head of him who owned them:
Ednyfed, King of Dyfed,
His head was borne before us;
His wine and beasts supplied our feasts,
And his overthrow, our chorus.

Thomas Love Peacock

Break of Day in the Trenches

The darkness crumbles away.

It is the same old druid Time as ever,

Only a live thing leaps my hand,

A queer sardonic rat,

As I pull the parapet's poppy

To stick behind my ear.

Droll rat, they would shoot you if they knew

Your cosmopolitan sympathies.

Now you have touched this English hand

You will do the same to a German

Soon, no doubt, if it be your pleasure

To cross the sleeping green between.

It seems you inwardly grin as you pass

Strong eyes, fine limbs, haughty athletes,

Less chanced than you for life,

Bonds to the whims of murder,

Sprawled in the bowels of the earth,

The torn fields of France.

What do you see in our eyes

At the shrieking iron and flame

Hurled through still heavens?

What quaver — what heart aghast?

Poppies whose roots are in man's veins

Drop, and are ever dropping;

But mine in my ear is safe —

Just a little white with the dust.

Isaac Rosenberg

The General

"Good-morning, good-morning!" the General said
When we met him last week on our way to the line.
Now the soldiers he smiled at are most of 'em dead,
And we're cursing his staff for incompetent swine.
"He's a cheery old card," grunted Harry to Jack
As they slogged up to Arras with rifle and pack.

....

But he did for them both by his plan of attack.

Siegfried Sassoon

Death, Be Not Proud

Death, be not proud, though some have called thee
Mighty and dreadful, for thou art not so;
For those whom thou think'st thou dost overthrow
Die not, poor Death, nor yet canst thou kill me.
From Rest and Sleep, which but thy pictures be,
Much pleasure; then from thee much more must flow,
And soonest our best men with thee do go,
Rest of their bones, and soul's delivery.
Thou art slave to fate, chance, kings, and desperate men,
And dost with poison, war, and sickness dwell,
And poppy, or charms can make us sleep as well
And better than thy stroke; why swell'st thou then?
One short sleep past, we wake eternally,
And death shall be no more; death, thou shalt die.

John Donne

On His Blindness

When I consider how my light is spent

Ere half my days, in this dark world and wide,

And that one talent which is death to hide,

Lodged with me useless, though my soul more bent

To serve therewith my Maker, and present

My true account, lest he returning, chide;

"Doth God exact day-labor, light denied?"

I fondly ask: but Patience, to prevent

That murmur, soon replies, "God doth not need

Either man's work, or his own gifts; who best

Bear his mild yoke, they serve him best; his state

Is kingly: thousands at his bidding speed,

And post o'er land and ocean without rest;

They also serve who only stand and wait."

John Milton

High Flight

Oh! I have slipped the surly bonds of Earth

And danced the skies on laughter-silvered wings;

Sunward I've climbed, and joined the tumbling

    mirth

Of sun-split clouds — and done a hundred things

You have not dreamed of — wheeled and soared and

     swung

High in sunlit silence. Hov'ring there,

I've chased the shouting wind along, and flung

My eager craft through footless halls of air…

Up, up the long, delirious, burning blue

I've topped the wind-swept heights with easy grace

Where never lark, or even eagle flew —

And, while with silent, lifting mind I've trod

The high untrespassed sanctity of space,

Put out my hand, and touched the face of God.

John Gillespie Magee, Jr.

So We'll Go No More A-Roving

So we'll go no more a-roving
So late into the night,
Though the heart be still as loving,
And the moon be still as bright.

For the sword outwears its sheath,
And the soul wears out the breast,
And the heart must pause to breathe,
And love itself have rest.

Though the night was made for loving,
And the day returns too soon,
Yet we'll go no more a-roving
By the light of the moon.

George Gordon, Lord Byron

Jenny Kissed Me

Jenny kiss'd me when we met,
Jumping from the chair she sat in;
Time, you thief, who love to get
Sweets into your list, put that in!
Say I'm weary, say I'm sad,
Say that health and wealth have miss'd me,
Say I'm growing old, but add,
Jenny kiss'd me.

Leigh Hunt

Pad, Pad

I always remember your beautiful flowers
And the beautiful kimono you wore
When you sat on the couch
With that tigerish crouch
And told me you loved me no more.

What I cannot remember is how I felt when you were unkind
All I know is, if you were unkind now I should not mind.
Ah me, the power to feel exaggerated, angry and sad
The years have taken from me. Softly I go now, pad pad.

Stevie Smith

Burnt Offering

Because there was no wind,
The smoke of your letters hung in the air
For a long time;
And its shape
Was the shape of your face,
My Beloved.

Amy Lowell

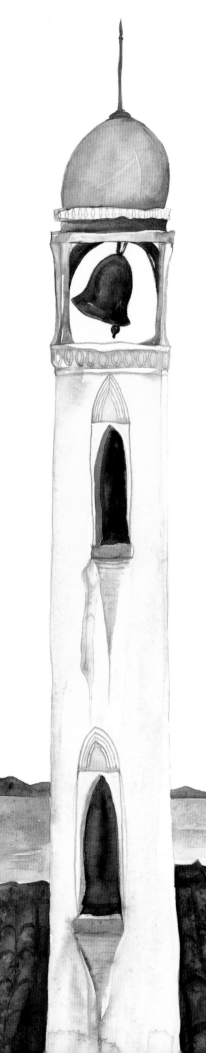

Meditation XVII

No man is an island, entire of itself;

Every man is a piece of the Continent, a part of the main.

If a clod be washed away by the sea, Europe is the less,

As well as if a promontory were;

Any man's death diminishes me,

Because I am involved in mankind.

And therefore never send to know for whom the bell tolls;

It tolls for thee.

John Donne

Song

Stop all the clocks, cut off the telephone,

Prevent the dog from barking with a juicy bone,

Silence the pianos and with muffled drum

Bring out the coffin, let the mourners come.

Let aeroplanes circle moaning overhead

Scribbling on the sky the message He Is Dead,

Put crêpe bows round the white necks of the public doves,

Let the traffic policemen wear black cotton gloves.

He was my North, my South, my East and West,

My working week and my Sunday rest,

My noon, my midnight, my talk, my song;

I thought that love would last for ever: I was wrong.

The stars are not wanted now: put out every one;

Pack up the moon and dismantle the sun;

Pour away the ocean and sweep up the wood;

For nothing now can ever come to any good.

W. H. Auden

Music

Let me go where'er I will

I hear a sky-born music still:

It sounds from all things old,

It sounds from all things young;

From all that's fair, from all that's foul,

Peals out a cheerful song.

It is not only in the bird,

Not only where the rainbow glows,

Nor in the song of woman heard,

But in the darkest, meanest things

There always, always, something sings.

'Tis not in the high stars alone,

Nor in the cups of budding flowers,

Nor in the redbreast's mellow tone,

Nor in the bow that smiles in showers,

But in the mud and scum and things

There always, always, something sings.

Ralph Waldo Emerson

My Heart Leaps Up

My heart leaps up when I behold
A rainbow in the sky:
So was it when my life began;
So is it now I am a man;
So be it when I shall grow old,
Or let me die!
The Child is father of the Man,
And I could wish my days to be
Bound each to each by natural piety.

William Wordsworth

from *The Man with the Blue Guitar*

One

The man bent over his guitar,
A shearsman of sorts. The day was green.

They said, "You have a blue guitar,
You do not play things as they are."

The man replied, "Things as they are
Are changed upon the blue guitar."

And they said to him, "But play, you must,
A tune beyond us, yet ourselves,

A tune upon the blue guitar,
Of things exactly as they are."

Two

I cannot bring a world quite round,
Although I patch it as I can.

I sing a hero's head, large eye
And bearded bronze, but not a man,

Although I patch him as I can
And reach through him almost to man.

If a serenade almost to man
Is to miss, by that, things as they are,

Say that it is the serenade
Of a man that plays a blue guitar.

Wallace Stevens

The Road Not Taken

Two roads diverged in a yellow wood,
And sorry I could not travel both
And be one traveler, long I stood
And looked down one as far as I could
To where it bent in the undergrowth;

Then took the other, as just as fair,
And having perhaps the better claim,
Because it was grassy and wanted wear;
Though as for that the passing there
Had worn them really about the same.

And both that morning equally lay
In leaves no step had trodden black.
Oh, I kept the first for another day!
Yet knowing how way leads on to way,
I doubted if I should ever come back.

I shall be telling this with a sigh
Somewhere ages and ages hence:
Two roads diverged in a wood, and I —
I took the one less traveled by,
And that has made all the difference.

Robert Frost

from *The Garden*

What wond'rous Life in this I lead!
Ripe Apples drop about my head;
The Luscious Clusters of the Vine
Upon my Mouth do crush their Wine;
The Nectaren, and curious Peach,
Into my hands themselves do reach;
Stumbling on melons, as I pass,
Insnar'd with Flow'rs, I fall on grass.

Mean while the Mind, from pleasure less,
Withdraws into its happiness:
The Mind, that Ocean where each kind
Does streight its own resemblance find;
Yet it creates, transcending these,
Far other Worlds, and other Seas,
Annihilating all that's made
To a green Thought in a green shade.

Andrew Marvell

If —

If you can keep your head when all about you

    Are losing theirs and blaming it on you;

If you can trust yourself when all men doubt you,

    But make allowance for their doubting too;

If you can wait and not be tired by waiting,

    Or, being lied about, don't deal in lies,

Or, being hated, don't give way to hating,

    And yet don't look too good, nor talk too wise;

If you can dream — and not make dreams your master;

    If you can think — and not make thoughts your aim;

If you can meet with Triumph and Disaster

    And treat those two imposters just the same;

If you can bear to hear the truth you've spoken

    Twisted by knaves to make a trap for fools,

Or watch the things you gave your life to, broken,

    And stoop and build 'em up with worn-out tools;

If you can make one heap of all your winnings

     And risk it on one turn of pitch-and-toss,

And lose, and start again at your beginnings

     And never breathe a word about your loss;

If you can force your heart and nerve and sinew

     To serve your turn long after they are gone,

And so hold on when there is nothing in you

     Except the Will which says to them: "Hold on!"

If you can talk with crowds and keep your virtue,

     Or walk with Kings — nor lose the common touch;

If neither foes nor loving friends can hurt you,

     If all men count with you, but none too much;

If you can fill the unforgiving minute

     With sixty seconds' worth of distance run —

Yours is the Earth and everything that's in it,

     And — which is more — you'll be a Man, my son!

Rudyard Kipling

The Highwayman

The wind was a torrent of darkness among the gusty trees.

The moon was a ghostly galleon tossed upon cloudy seas.

The road was a ribbon of moonlight over the purple moor,

And the highwayman came riding —

      Riding — riding —

The highwayman came riding, up to the old inn-door.

He'd a French cocked-hat on his forehead, a bunch of lace at his chin,

A coat of the claret velvet, and breeches of brown doe-skin.

They fitted with never a wrinkle: his boots were up to the thigh.

And he rode with a jeweled twinkle,

      His pistol butts a-twinkle,

His rapier hilt a-twinkle, under the jeweled sky.

Over the cobbles he clattered and clashed in the dark inn-yard.

He tapped with his whip on the shutters, but all was locked and barred.

He whistled a tune to the window, and who should be waiting there

But the landlord's black-eyed daughter,

      Bess, the landlord's daughter,

Plaiting a dark red love-knot into her long black hair.

And dark in the dark old inn-yard a stable-wicket creaked

Where Tim the ostler listened; his face was white and peaked;

His eyes were hollows of madness, his hair was mouldy hay,

But he loved the landlord's daughter,

      The landlord's red-lipped daughter.

Dumb as a dog he listened, and he heard the robber say —

"One kiss, my bonny sweetheart, I'm after a prize tonight,

But I shall be back with the yellow gold before the morning light;

Yet, if they press me sharply, and harry me through the day,

Then look for me by moonlight,

      Watch for me by moonlight,

I'll come to thee by moonlight, though hell should bar the way."

He rose upright in the stirrups. He scarce could reach her hand,

But she loosened her hair in the casement. His face burnt like a brand

As the black cascade of perfume came tumbling over his breast;

And he kissed its waves in the moonlight,

      (O, sweet black waves in the moonlight!)

Then he tugged at his rein in the moonlight, and galloped away to the west.

He did not come in the dawning. He did not come at noon;

And out of the tawny sunset, before the rise of the moon,

When the road was a gypsy's ribbon, looping the purple moor,

A red-coat troop came marching —

      Marching — marching —

King George's men came marching, up to the old inn-door.

They said no word to the landlord. They drank his ale instead.

But they gagged his daughter, and bound her, to the foot of her narrow bed.

Two of them knelt at her casement, with muskets at their side.

There was death at every window;

      And hell at one dark window;

For Bess could see, through her casement, the road that *he* would ride.

They had tied her up to attention, with many a sniggering jest.

They had bound a musket beside her, with the muzzle beneath her breast.

"Now keep good watch!" and they kissed her. She heard the doomed man say —

Look for me by moonlight;

      Watch for me by moonlight;

I'll come to thee by moonlight, though hell should bar the way!

She twisted her hands behind her; but all the knots held good.

She writhed her hands till her fingers were wet with sweat or blood.

They stretched and strained in the darkness, and the hours crawled by like years,

Till, now, on the stroke of midnight,

      Cold, on the stroke of midnight,

The tip of one finger touched it! The trigger at least was hers!

117

The tip of one finger touched it. She strove no more for the rest.

Up, she stood to attention, with the muzzle beneath her breast.

She would not risk their hearing; she would not strive again;

For the road lay bare in the moonlight;

      Blank and bare in the moonlight;

And the blood of her veins, in the moonlight, throbbed to her love's refrain.

Tlot-tlot; tlot-tlot! Had they heard it? The horse hoofs ringing clear;

Tlot-tlot, tlot-tlot, in the distance? Were they deaf that they did not hear?

Down the ribbon of moonlight, over the brow of the hill,

The highwayman came riding —

      Riding — riding —

The red-coats looked to their priming! She stood up, straight and still.

Tlot-tlot, in the frosty silence! *Tlot-tlot,* in the echoing night!

Nearer he came and nearer. Her face was like a light.

Her eyes grew wide for a moment; she drew one last deep breath,

Then her finger moved in the moonlight,

      Her musket shattered the moonlight,

Shattered her breast in the moonlight and warned him — with her death.

He turned; he spurred to the west; he did not know who stood

Bowed, with her head o'er the musket, drenched with her own blood!

Not till the dawn he heard it, and his face grew grey to hear

How Bess, the landlord's daughter,

      The landlord's black-eyed daughter

Had watched for her love in the moonlight, and died in the darkness there.

Back, he spurred like a madman, shouting a curse to the sky,

With the white road smoking behind him and his rapier brandished high.

Blood-red were his spurs in the golden noon; wine-red was his velvet coat;

When they shot him down on the highway,

   Down like a dog on the highway,

And he lay in his blood on the highway, with the bunch of lace at his throat.

And still of a winter's night, they say, when the wind is in the trees,

When the moon is a ghostly galleon tossed upon cloudy seas,

When the road is a ribbon of moonlight over the purple moor,

A highwayman comes riding —

   Riding — riding —

A highwayman comes riding, up to the old inn-door.

Over the cobbles he clatters and clangs in the dark inn-yard.

He taps with his whip on the shutters, but all is locked and barred.

He whistles a tune to the window, and who should be waiting there

But the landlord's black-eyed daughter.

   Bess, the landlord's daughter,

Plaiting a dark red love-knot into her long black hair.

Alfred Noyes

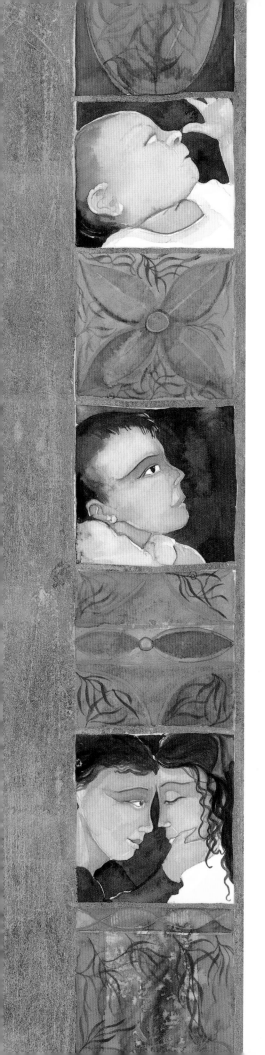

All the World's a Stage

All the world's a stage,
And all the men and women merely players.
They have their exits and their entrances;
And one man in his time plays many parts,
His acts being seven ages. At first the infant,
Mewling and puking in the nurse's arms.
Then the whining schoolboy, with his satchel
And shining morning face, creeping like snail
Unwillingly to school. And then the lover,
Sighing like furnace, with a woeful ballad
Made to his mistress's eyebrow. Then a soldier,
Full of strange oaths, and bearded like the pard,
Jealous in honour, sudden and quick in quarrel,
Seeking the bubble reputation

Even in the cannon's mouth. And then the justice,
In fair round belly with good capon lined,
With eyes severe and beard of formal cut,
Full of wise saws and modern instances;
And so he plays his part. The sixth age shifts
Into the lean and slippered pantaloon,
With spectacles on nose and pouch on side,
His youthful hose, well saved, a world too wide
For his shrunk shank; and his big manly voice,
Turning again toward childish treble, pipes
And whistles in his sound. Last scene of all,
That ends this strange, eventful history,
Is second childishness and mere oblivion,
Sans teeth, sans eyes, sans taste, sans everything.

William Shakespeare

The Poet's Song

The rain had fallen, the Poet arose,
    He passed by the town, and out of the street,
A light wind blew from the gates of the sun,
    And waves of shadow went over the wheat,
And he sat him down in a lonely place,
    And chanted a melody loud and sweet,
That made the wild-swan pause in her cloud,
    And the lark drop down at his feet.

The swallow stopt as he hunted the fly,
    The snake slipt under a spray,
The hawk stood with the down on his beak,
    And stared, with his foot on the prey,
And the nightingale thought, "I have sung many songs,
    But never a one so gay,
For he sings of what the world will be
    When the years have died away."

Alfred, Lord Tennyson

First Lines

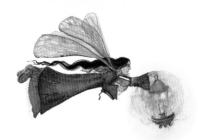

Acknowledgments

"Song" copyright © 1939 & renewed 1967 by W. H. Auden, "The Night Mail" copyright © 1938 by W. H. Auden, from *Collected Poems* by W. H. Auden. Used by permission of Random House, Inc.

"maggie and milly and molly and may". Copyright © 1956, 1984, 1991 by the Trustees for the E. E. Cummings Trust, from *Complete Poems: 1904 – 1962* by E. E. Cummings, edited by George J. Firmage. Used by permission of Liveright Publishing Corporation.

"The Beautiful" by W. H. Davies reprinted by permission of Mrs. H. M. Davies Will Trust, Dee & Griffin.

Samuel French Ltd for "Moonlit Apples" by John Drinkwater.

"Cats" by Eleanor Farjeon from *Blackbird Has Spoken* published by Macmillan. Reprinted by permission of David Higham Associates.

"Something told the wild geese" by Rachel Field reprinted with the permission of Simon & Schuster Books for Young Readers, an imprint of Simon & Schuster Children's Publishing Division from *Poems* by Rachel Field. Copyright 1934 Macmillan Publishing Company; copyright renewed © 1958 Arthur S. Pederson.

"Dreams" from *The Collected Poems of Langston Hughes* by Langston Hughes, copyright © 1994 by The Estate of Langston Hughes. Used by permission of Alfred A. Knopf, a division of Random House, Inc.

"The Wild Trees" by Laurie Lee. Reprinted by permission of PDF on behalf of The Estate of Laurie Lee © 1960.

"Furry Bear" from *Now We Are Six* by A. A. Milne, copyright 1927 by E. P. Dutton, renewed © 1955 by A. A. Milne. Used by permission of Dutton Childrens Books, A Division of Penguin Young Readers Group, A Member of Penguin Group (USA) Inc., 345 Hudson Street, New York, NY 10014. All rights reserved.

"The Fish" by Marianne Moore. Reprinted with the permission of Scribner, an imprint of Simon & Schuster Adult Publishing Group, from *Collected Poems* by Marianne Moore. Copyright © 1935 by Marianne Moore; copyright renewed © 1963 by Marianne Moore and T. S. Eliot.

"Morning Song" by Sylvia Plath reprinted by permission of HarperCollins Publishers. Copyright © 1961 by Ted Hughes.

"Spell of Creation" by Kathleen Raine reprinted by permission of Brian Keeble, Literary Executor of the Estate of Kathleen Raine.

"The Paintbox" by E. V. Rieu reprinted by permission of the Authors Licensing & Collecting Society Ltd on behalf of the estate of the late E. V. Rieu.

"Pad, Pad" by Stevie Smith, from *Collected Poems of Stevie Smith*, copyright © 1972 by Stevie Smith. Reprinted by permission of New Directions Publishing Corp.

"The Man with the Blue Guitar" by Wallace Stevens from *The Collected Poems of Wallace Stevens* by Wallace Stevens, copyright © 1954 by Wallace Stevens and renewed 1982 by Holly Stevens. Used by permission of Alfred A. Knopf, a division of Random House, Inc.

"Fern Hill" by Dylan Thomas, from *The Poems of Dylan Thomas*, copyright © 1945 by The Trustees for the Copyrights of Dylan Thomas. Reprinted by permission of New Directions Publishing Corp.

"Oliphaunt", from *The Adventures of Tom Bombadil* by J. R. R. Tolkien. Copyright © 1962, 1990 by Unwin Hyman Ltd. Copyright © renewed 1990 by Christopher R. Tolkien, John F. R. Tolkien and Priscilla M. A. R. Tolkien. Reprinted by permission of Houghton Mifflin Co. All rights reserved.

"Dorothy Dances" by Louis Untermeyer. Permission is granted by arrangement with the Estate of Louise Untermeyer, Norma Anchin Untermeyer c/o Professional Publishing Services. The reprint is granted with the expressed permission by Laurence S. Untermeyer.

"This Is Just To Say" by William Carlos Williams, from *Collected Poems: 1909-1939, Volume I*, copyright © 1938 by New Directions Publishing Corp. Reprinted by permission of New Directions Publishing Corp.

"The Stolen Child", "The Wild Swans at Coole" and "He Wishes for the Cloths of Heaven" by W. B. Yeats reprinted with the permission of Scribner, an imprint of Simon & Schuster Adult Publishing Group, from *The Collected Poems of W. B. Yeats, Volume I: The Poems, Revised*, edited by Richard J. Finneran. (New York: Scribner, 1997).

Dreams

Hold fast to dreams
For if dreams die
Life is a broken-winged bird
That cannot fly.